Who Are YOU?

31 Names from the Holy Scriptures
to Remind You that You are
God's Prized Creation

Merle M. Mills

Content design by Evelyn J. Wagoner

ISBN #:13:978-0-9886 162-2-6

Acknowledgements

To my God, thank You for loving me
and forgiving me.
As long as You give me breath,
I will serve You.

To my family, thank you for supporting me
by giving me the freedom of many hours
at my computer.

To those who generously support,
share your God-given talents, and pray for me,
thank you.

Contents

INTRODUCTION

For years, I had no idea of my true identity until I began to read what my Heavenly Father said about me in the Holy Scriptures. Those truths freed me from the opinion of others and changed my life in such a powerful way that I desired to share them with those who would dare to read—and dare to believe—them.

If you have picked up this book, it is your time for transformation. My prayer is that as you read each page and memorize what our Heavenly Father says about you, you will discover who you are: valuable ... precious ... special ... God's prized creation.

Your Name
TEMPLE

In Scripture, the definition of the word *TEMPLE* is *GOD'S DWELLING PLACE*. When we choose a relationship with Jesus Christ, our bodies become His dwelling place. His temple is a place that is sacred, a place where worship takes place, where strength is gained. A place where miracles happen and lives are changed. Knowing we are God's temple will cause us to treat our bodies with great respect and significance.

Don't you know that you are God's temple and that God's Spirit lives in you?[1] Don't you realize that your body is the temple of the Holy Spirit, who lives in you and was given to you by God? You do not belong to yourself.[2] For we are the temple of the living God. As God said: "I will live in them and walk among them, I will be their God, and they will be My people."[3] We are carefully joined together in Him, becoming a holy temple for the Lord.[4]

References:
[1]1 Corinthians 3:16 (GW); [2]1 Corinthians 6:19;
[3]2 Corinthians 6:16b; [4]Ephesians 2:21

Your Name
FREE

When we accept and believe the truth of the names our Heavenly Father calls us, we begin to experience freedom from the stigma of names others have called us, and names we have called ourselves.

In this passage, John records the words Jesus spoke regarding promised freedom through Himself. One definition of the word *FREE* in the original translation of this passage is *TO CAUSE SOMEONE TO RECEIVE FREEDOM.* Jesus came to set us free and to cause us to receive freedom. Will you receive that freedom today? It's yours for the asking.

So if the Son sets you free, you are truly free.[1] Christ has truly set us free.[2] For the LORD has anointed Me to bring good news to the poor. He has sent Me to comfort the brokenhearted and to proclaim that captives will be released and prisoners will be freed.[3] And because you belong to Him, the power of the life-giving Spirit has freed you from the power of sin that leads to death.[4] The truth will set you free.[5]

References:
[1]John 8:36; [2]Galatians 5:1
[3]Isaiah 61:1; [4]Romans 8:2; [5]John 8:32

Your Name
CALLED

There is a certain ring to the sound of one's name being called by a loved one or a friend. This promise from Scripture tells us through the voice of Isaiah the prophet that God calls us by name.

Before beginning each day, take a few quiet moments to listen to God's voice as He calls your name. Read the Scripture references below. Might this be your prayer? "*Heavenly Father, thank You for knowing me and for calling me by my name. I will say yes to Your call, in Jesus' name, amen.*" It may be the most vital moment of your day.

See how very much our Father loves us, for He calls us His children and that is what we are![1] And having chosen them, He called them to come to Him. And having called them, He gave them right standing with Himself.[2] For as members of one body you are called to live in peace.[3] For I am called by Your name, O LORD God of hosts.[4] I have called you by name.[5]

References:
[1] 1 John 3:1; [2] Romans 8:30
[3] Colossians 3:15; [4] Jeremiah 15:16 (KJV)
[5] Isaiah 43:1b

Your Name
DELIGHT

In this passage, one of the meanings of the word *DELIGHT* is *TO BE PLEASED WITH*. Many times our relationships with others and their being pleased with us is based upon whether or not we live up to their expectations. We may even transfer that trend of thought to our relationship with our Heavenly Father. God's delight for, or His being pleased with us, is not based on how we see ourselves or how others see us, but on His unconditional and "unfailing love." (Psalm 36:5)

Today, as you read these Words from the Holy Scriptures, be convinced that God calls you His delight and is pleased with you.

He led me to a place of safety. He rescued me because He delights in me.[1] Never again will you be called "The Forsaken City" or "The Desolate Land." Your new name will be "The City of God's Delight" and "The Bride of God," for the LORD delights in you and will claim you as His bride.[2] The LORD your God among you is powerful—He will save and He will take joyful delight in you. In His love He will renew you with His love; He will celebrate with singing because of you.[3] The LORD directs the steps of the godly. He delights in every detail of their lives.[4]

References:
[1]Psalm 18:19; [2]Isaiah 62:4; [3]Zephaniah 3:17
[4]Psalm 37:23

Your Name

HEIR

In this passage, the word *HEIR* is translated *ONE WHO TAKES POSSESSION OF OR INHERITS*. When we accept Jesus Christ into our lives, we inherit the richness of His name that no longer identifies us as less than our worth and value. We become an heir to the names of the One whose we have become. This invites us to accept all His name represents. Claim your inheritance today.

And since we are His children, we are His heirs. In fact, together with Christ we are heirs of God's glory. But if we are to share His glory, we must also share His suffering.[1] Furthermore, because we are united with Christ, we have received an inheritance from God, for He chose us in advance, and He makes everything work out according to His plan.[2] And we have a priceless inheritance—an inheritance that is kept in heaven for you, pure and undefiled, beyond the reach of change and decay.[3] God has made you His heir.[4]

References:
[1]Romans 8:17; [2]Ephesians 1:11;
[3]1 Peter 1:4; [4]Galatians 4:7b

Your Name
STRONG

Life can be filled with challenges: health, relationships, family, and financial, to name a few. Another name God calls us is *strong*. We therefore have the ability and strength to overcome these challenges. David was victorious against the giant saying, *"I come to you in the name of the Lord of Heaven's Armies."* (I Samuel 17:45) It is in His name and with His strength we have been named. We have His ability and His strength to face and overcome life's challenges.

For I can do everything through Christ who gives me strength.[1] The LORD is the strength of my life; of whom shall I be afraid?[2] Don't be afraid, for I am with you. Don't be discouraged, for I am your God. I will strengthen you and help you. I will hold you up with My victorious right hand.[3] The people that do know their God shall be strong, and do exploits.[4]

References:
[1]Philippians 4:13; [2]Psalm 27:1 (KJV)
[3]Isaiah 41:10; [4]Daniel 11:32 (KJV)

Your Name

ACCEPTED

Have you ever felt unacceptable because of education, finances, age, or culture? God's acceptance of you does not depend on any of these things. Whatever your status in life, God loves you, cares for you, and has great plans for you. God created you and accepts you just as you are.

He has made us accepted in the Beloved.[1] "Come now, let's settle this," says the LORD. "Though your sins are like scarlet, I will make them as white as snow. Though they are red like crimson, I will make them as white as wool."[2] In every nation He accepts those who fear Him and do what is right.[3] I will never turn away anyone who comes to Me.[4]

References:
[1]Ephesians 1:6 (KJV); [2]Isaiah 1:18
[3]Acts 10:35; [4]John 6:37 (GW)

Your Name
BEAUTIFUL

By today's standards, qualification for beauty focuses much on outward appearance. Your beauty is unique and is based on the inner well of beauty our God has placed on the inside of you. It is not based on your comparison to others, but on the Truth of what your Creator says about you.

People judge by outward appearance, but the Lord looks at the heart.[1] I will give thanks to You because I have been so amazingly and miraculously made. Your works are miraculous, and my soul is fully aware of this.[2] You are beautiful, my darling, like the lovely city of Tirzah. Yes, as beautiful as Jerusalem, as majestic as an army with billowing banners.[3] Look at you! You are so beautiful, my true love! Look at you! You are so beautiful! Your eyes are like doves![4]

References:
[1] 1 Samuel 16:7; [2] Psalm 139:14 (GW);
[3] Song of Solomon 6:4; [4] Song of Solomon 1:15 (GW)

Your Name
TREASURE

One of the Hebrew definitions of the word *TREASURE* is *JEWELS*. Treasure can include precious stones, costly gems, and valuable gold coins. It doesn't matter how you see yourself or how others perceive you; God calls you His treasure. Remind yourself of this name often. Who are you? You are of value, a treasure and a jewel, says the Master.

You have been set apart as holy to the Lord your God, and He has chosen you from all the nations of the earth to be His own special treasure.[1] Now if you will obey Me and keep My covenant, you will be My own special treasure from among all the peoples on earth; for all the earth belongs to Me.[2] "They will be My people," says the Lord of Heaven's Armies. "On the day when I act in judgment, they will be My own special treasure." [3] Our bodies are made of clay, yet we have the treasure of the Good News in them. This shows that the superior power of this treasure belongs to God and doesn't come from us.[4]

References:
[1]Deuteronomy 14:2; [2]Exodus 19:5;
[3]Malachi 3:17; [4]2 Corinthians 4:7 (GW)

Your Name

PRECIOUS

One of the definitions given by Webster's online dictionary for the word *PRECIOUS* is OF GREAT VALUE OR HIGH PRICE. The word PRECIOUS is also often used when speaking about diamonds, gold, and other costly stones. Recently, the price of gold has skyrocketed, and many are exchanging theses gems for cash value. Your worth and value is not based on a fluctuating index scale. Neither is it based on the fluctuating opinions of yours or of others. It is based on the never-changing Word of God, which says you are precious. By faith, believe it and accept it.

Since you are precious and honored in My sight, and because I love you, I will give people in exchange for you, nations in exchange for your life[1] **You are** *more precious than rubies.[2] Your faith is more precious than gold.[3] You are very precious to God.[4]*

References:
[1]Isaiah 43:4 (NIV); [2]Proverbs 31:10 [emphasis mine]
[3]1 Peter 1:7b (GW); [4]Daniel 9:23b;

Your Name
SPECIAL

When God sent the prophet Samuel to the home of Jesse to choose a king, Jesse's youngest son, David, was in the field taking care of sheep (1 Samuel 17). David's brothers seemed to be qualified to wear the crown, and none—including his father—felt David was the choice. While we may not be identified as special, even by family members or by those close to us, believe and know this:

The Lord will not reject His people; He will not abandon His own special possession.[1] He gave Himself for us to set us free from every sin and to cleanse us so that we can be His special people who are enthusiastic about doing good things.[3] The Lord God has chosen you to be His own special treasure.[3]

References:
[1]Psalm 94:14; [2]Titus 2:14 (GW)
[3]Deuteronomy 7:6

Your Name

VALUABLE

Because of their value, gold jewelry, important documents, diamonds, and expensive chinaware are often placed in safety deposit boxes, cabinets, or treasure chests. We tend to care for them in a more painstaking way. Live today knowing that your value and worth are not based on the opinion of others, or on the opinion you have of yourself, but on words from the Holy Scriptures spoken by the One who created you and gave you the gift of life ... the One who gives you value, cares for, watches over you in a meticulous way, and places you in Heaven's list of treasures.

What is mankind that You are mindful of them, human beings that You care for them? You have made them a little lower than the angels and crowned them with glory and honor.[1] Look at the birds. They don't plant or harvest or store food in barns, for your heavenly Father feeds them. And aren't you far more valuable to Him than they are?[2] And the very hairs on your head are all numbered. So don't be afraid; you are more valuable to God than a whole flock of sparrows.[3]

References:
[1]Psalm 8:4-5 (NIV); [2]Matthew 6:26;
[3]Luke 12:7

Your Name
RIGHTEOUS

A relationship with Jesus Christ transforms us from unrighteousness to righteousness. The word used here in the New Testament of the Bible means THE STATE OF BEING IN A PROPER RELATIONSHIP WITH GOD. Do you feel righteous or that you are in a proper relationship with God all the time? Probably not. However, the fact is you are. Reading these Scripture references often, and memorizing them, will build faith and help replace those lingering feelings of doubt.

God made Him who had no sin to be sin for us, so that in Him we might become the righteousness of God.[1] Then all Your people will be righteous, and they will possess the land forever.[2] You are partners with Christ Jesus because of God. Jesus has become our wisdom sent from God, our righteousness, our holiness, and our ransom from sin.[3] I am overwhelmed with joy in the Lord my God! For He has dressed me with the clothing of salvation and draped me in a robe of righteousness.[4]

References:
[1]2 Corinthians 5:21 (NIV); [2]Isaiah 60:21a (NIV)
[3] 1 Corinthians 1:30 (GW); [4]Isaiah 61:10

Your Name
FEARFULLY AND WONDERFULLY MADE

A HEART PUMPS THE EQUIVALENT OF ABOUT 75 GALLONS OF BLOOD THROUGH THE BODY IN EVERY HOUR. DOING SUCH A SIMPLE THING AS LIFTING A SPOONFUL OF SOUP TO ONE'S MOUTH INVOLVES MORE THAN 30 JOINTS AND 50 MUSCLES, ALL OF THEM FUNCTIONING TOGETHER IN PERFECTLY SYNCHRONIZED ORDER. THE LENS OF THE EYE IS HELD IN POSITION BY A RING-SHAPED MUSCLE WHICH BOTH CONTRACTS AND EXPANDS THE LENS AND THEREBY ACCOMMODATES VISION OF DISTANCE.[1] I am not medical person; however, to me, these facts certainly indicate the fear and wonder invested by our Heavenly Father in making His most prized creation, you and me. Today, take a moment, and celebrate who you are. You are fearfully and wonderfully made!

Then the LORD God formed the man from the dust of the ground. He breathed the breath of life into the man's nostrils, and the man became a living person.[2] I praise You because I am fearfully and wonderfully made.[3] For we are God's handiwork.[4] For the Spirit of God has made me, and the breath of the Almighty gives me life.[5] You made me; You created me. Now give me the sense to follow Your commands.[6]

References: [1]The Wonders of Creation; [2]Genesis 2:7; [3]Psalm 139:14a (NIV); [4]Ephesians 2:10a (NIV); [5]Job 33:4; [6]Psalm 119:73

Your Name

FORGIVEN

I FORGIVE YOU are three words that, when spoken in sincerity, mean much to one who has been wronged or who has wronged another. Spoken from our Heavenly Father, these words will change your life forever. If you have a past sin that still hinders you from living in freedom through God's forgiveness, you no longer have to be burdened with feelings of condemnation. Place it at the Savior's feet, ask for His forgiveness. Accept that you are forgiven, then find and fulfill the great plan and purpose our God has for your life.

He forgives all my sins and heals all my diseases.[1] And Jesus said unto her, "Neither do I condemn you: go, and sin no more."[2] Who is a God like You? You forgive sin and overlook the rebellion of Your faithful people. You will not be angry forever, because You would rather show mercy.[3] "Be encouraged, My child! Your sins are forgiven."[4]

References:
[1]Psalm 103:3; [2]John 8:11b (KJV)
[3]Micah 7:18 (GW); [4]Matthew 9:2b

Your Name

WISE

Normally, when we think of a wise person, we picture someone with a long, white beard, wearing horn-rimmed glasses, and living on a high, mountain peak. One definition given by Webster's Dictionary for the word WISE is HAVING A CAPACITY FOR SOUND JUDGMENT MARKED BY DEEP UNDERSTANDING. In Scripture, God is referred to as the only wise God (Jude 1:25, 1 Timothy 1:17, Romans 16:27). Our relationship with Jesus Christ qualifies us to be called wise. This name that says, in Him, you and I are given the ability to apply wisdom to every action, every decision, every situation, and every circumstance in our lives.

Jesus has become our wisdom sent from God.[1] He has showered His kindness on us, along with all wisdom and understanding.[2] He gives wisdom to the wise and knowledge to the scholars.[3] For I will give you the right words and such wisdom that none of your opponents will be able to reply or refute you![4] You are wise in Christ.[5] I will give you a wise and understanding heart such as no one else has had or ever will have![6]

References:
[1]1 Corinthians 1:30 (GW); [2]Ephesians 1:8
[3]Daniel 2:21; [4]Luke 21:15
[5]1 Corinthians 4:10 (KJV); [6]I Kings 3:12

Your Name

APPLE OF GOD'S EYE

The eyeball, or globe of the eye, with pupil in center, called "apple" from its round shape. Its great value and careful protection by the eyelids automatically closing when there is the least possibility of danger made it the emblem of that which was most precious and jealously protected.[1]

Being called *"the apple of God's eye"* is another example of our preciousness and value, comparing us with the preciousness of the eyes, and demonstrates the extreme protection, care, and provision with which you were created.

Whoever touches you touches the apple of His eye.[2] Keep me as the apple of Your eye; hide me in the shadow of Your wings.[3] He shielded him and cared for him; He guarded him as the apple of His eye.[4]

References:
[1]International Standard Bible Encyclopedia
[2]Zechariah 2:8 (NIV); [3]Psalm 17:8 (NIV);
[4]Deuteronomy 32:10c (NIV)

Your Name
BOLD

The more time we spend studying the Scriptures, the more we will grow in our relationship with Jesus Christ. We will then realize how much He cares for us, and we become another name He has called us: bold and fearless. No longer are we timid, shy, or afraid. Why? Because we begin to understand we have the Greater One living in us (1 John 4:4). You have the boldness to fulfill and achieve your God-given dreams.

And so, dear brothers and sisters, we can boldly enter heaven's Most Holy Place because of the blood of Jesus.[1] Because of Christ and our faith in Him, we can now come boldly and confidently into God's presence.[2] So let us come boldly to the throne of our gracious God. There we will receive His mercy, and we will find grace to help us when we need it most.[3] The godly are bold as lions.[4]

References:
[1]Hebrews 10:19; [2]Ephesians 3:12
[3]Hebrews 4:16; [4]Proverbs 28:1

Your Name
MASTERPIECE

When you hear the word MASTERPIECE does Leonardo da Vinci's *Mona Lisa* come to mind? According to John Litchfield, it is *"the best known, the most visited, the most written about, the most sung about, the most parodied work of art in the world."* God calls you and me MASTERPIECE. Your brain in itself is a masterpiece. As Dr. Ben Carson states, *"we cannot overload the human brain. This divinely created brain has fourteen billion cells. If used to the maximum, this human computer inside our heads could contain all the knowledge of humanity from the beginning of the world to the present and still have room left over."*

This information is beyond imagination. In God's eyes, we are a perfect masterpiece. Look into a mirror today and say hello to the world's most acclaimed masterpiece, you!

I will give thanks to You because I have been so amazingly and miraculously made. Your works are miraculous, and my soul is fully aware of this.[1] You made me; You created me. Now give me the sense to follow Your commands.[2] For we are God's masterpiece![3]

References:
[1]Psalms 139:14 (GW) [2]Psalm 119:73
[3]Ephesians 2:10

Your Name
FRIEND

A friend forgives. A friend is patient. A friend protects. A friend takes time to know you. A friend is kind. True friendship with our Heavenly Father offers all these benefits. In addition, the relationship is everlasting. The true meaning of friendship with God is found in the pages of the Holy Scriptures. Read, study, and memorize what they say about this friendship. Then proclaim those words daily. I guarantee your life will be transformed as you begin to understand you have a friend who will be with you, *"even to the end of the age."* (Matthew 28:20) These words have transformed my life, and I am sure they will transform yours.

For since our friendship with God was restored by the death of His Son while we were still His enemies, we will certainly be saved through the life of His Son.[1] Wicked people are detestable to the Lord, but He offers His friendship to the godly.[2] There is no greater love than to lay down one's life for one's friends.[3] Now you are My friends, since I have told you everything the Father told Me.[4] The LORD is a friend to those who fear Him. He teaches them His covenant.[5]

References:
[1]Romans 5:10: [2]Proverbs 3:32
[3]John 15:13; [4]John 15:15; [5]Psalm 25:14

Your Name
MY PEOPLE

I had heard for years that God's desire was to have a personal relationship with me. I did not fully understand this until I began to spend time reading and studying Scripture. Then these words came alive to me: "*They will be my people, and I will be their God.*" They can come alive to you also. Insert your name in place of the words "they" and "their." The promise becomes yours.

_____ *will be My people, and I will be* _____ *'s God.*[1] *I will make My home among* _____. *I will be* _____ *'s God, and* _____ *will be My people.*[2] *Because He is our God, and we are the people in His care.*[3] *As God said: "I will live in them and walk among them. I will be their God, and they will be My people."*[4]

References:
[1]Jeremiah 32:38; [2]Ezekiel 37:27;
[3]Psalm 95:7 (GW); [4]2 Corinthians 6:16c

Your Name
LIGHT OF THE WORLD

Light dispels darkest midnight. With light, we read books, write essays, eat crispy egg rolls, entertain family and friends, perform household chores, and earn a living. It guides us through traffic. It gives life to plant and animal life. Light is vital to all life. In Scripture, Jesus referred to Himself as the *"Light of the World."* (John 9:5) He then tells us that we are *"lights of the world"* (Matthew 5:14). We have the ability to influence life around us. As William Barclay wrote, *"It may well be said that this is the greatest compliment that was ever paid to the individual Christian."* Who are you? You are the light of the world.

God rescued me from the grave, and now my life is filled with light.[1] For once you were full of darkness, but now you have light from the Lord. So live as people of light![2] For you are all children of the light and of the day; we don't belong to darkness and night.[3] You are the light of the world.[4]

References:
[1]Job 33:28; [2]Ephesians 5:8;
[3]1 Thessalonians 5:5; [4]Matthew 5:14a

Your Name

BELOVED

We all have been called names of endearment by grandparents, parents, siblings, and teachers (to name a few). One definition given in Webster's Dictionary for ENDEARMENT is A WORD OR AN ACT EXPRESSING AFFECTION. *In Scripture, the word beloved is a term of endearment used by our Heavenly Father to express His tender love for His chosen ones.[1]* This name—BELOVED—that we are called reminds you and me of God's great affection for the relationship we share.

"My beloved is mine and I am His.[2] "I am my beloved's and my beloved is mine.[3] "I belong to my beloved, and His desire is for me.[4] So stand fast in the Lord, my dearly beloved.[5]

References:
[1]International Standard Bible Encyclopedia;
[2]Song of Solomon 2:16a (NIV);
[3]Song of Solomon 6:3 (KJV);
[4]Song of Solomon 7:10 (NIV);
[5]Philippians 4:1 (KJV)

Your Name
HOLY

You may have been called names you have never shared with anyone. Names that have affected your self-image for years. Today, listen to the voice of your Heavenly Father as He calls you HOLY. *Anything that is holy is set apart. It is removed from the realm of the common and moved to the sphere of the sacred.[1]* Yes, it's talking about you. According to your Heavenly Father, you are moved from the common to the sacred. Replace any previous negative names you were called with the name HOLY.

I am the Lord who makes you holy[2]. "For you are a holy people, who belong to the Lord your God."[3] You are holy and blameless as you stand before Him without a single fault.[4] Even before He made the world, God loved us and chose us in Christ to be holy and without fault in His eyes.[5]

References:
[1]Expository Dictionary of Bible Words;
[2]Leviticus 20:8b; [3]Deuteronomy 7:6;
[4]Colossians 1:22c; [5]Ephesians 1:4;

Your Name

CHOSEN

You didn't choose Me. I chose you.[1] Before I was born, the Lord chose me. While I was in my mother's womb, He recorded my name.[2] Even before He made the world, God loved us and chose us in Christ to be holy and without fault in His eyes.[3] We know, dear brothers and sisters, that God loves you and has chosen you to be His own people.[4] For I have chosen you, says the Lord of hosts.[5]

We too choose names for our children before they are born. Sometimes the names we choose are names of those we deem to be great, famous, or influential. These words from Scripture demonstrate God personally choosing you. You were chosen by Him before you were born ... while you were in your mother's womb.

We are specially chosen, and named by—and for—the greatest One of all, the Creator of the universe and of life itself.

References:
[1]John 15:16; [2]Isaiah 49:1b (GW);
[3]Ephesians 1:4; [4]1 Thessalonians 1:4;
[5]Haggai 2:23 (KJV)

Your Name

CONQUEROR

When faced with challenges in life, we may be tempted to retreat, give in, or become depressed. Nowhere in the Scriptures are we prepared for defeat. Instead, we are called and prepared to be conquerors.

One definition of the word CONQUEROR given by Webster's Dictionary is TO WIN BY OVERCOMING OBSTACLES OR OPPOSITION. Whatever challenges you may face, you have power within you from the One who calls you conqueror, enabling you to overcome obstacles or opposition. You are called to win because you are a conqueror.

We are more than conquerors through Him that loved us.[1] I give unto you power to tread on serpents and scorpions, and over all the power of the enemy: and nothing shall by any means hurt you.[2] The Spirit who lives in you is greater than the spirit who lives in the world.[3]

References:
[1]Romans 8:37 (KJV); [2]Luke 10:19 (KJV);
[3]1 John 4:4c

Your Name

HONORED

The word HONORED suggests IMPORTANCE.[1] You are so important to God that no one else in the world was created with your fingerprint. In a crowded room, you may feel alone and unnoticed. However, you stand out and are noticed by God—and He honors you.

I will rescue and honor them.[2] The Father will honor anyone who serves Me.[3] You ... crowned them with glory and honor.[4] You are honored and I love you.[5]

References:
[1]Vine's Concise Dictionary of the Bible;
[2]Psalm 91:15; [3]John 12:26b;
[4]Hebrews 2:7; [5]Isaiah 43:4b

Your Name
BLESSED

God blesses you and you are blessed. TO BLESS in Scripture is translated TO SPEAK WELL OF. To be blessed is also translated to be HAPPY or FORTUNATE. Regardless of what others have called you, or what you have called yourself, your Heavenly Father speaks well of you. Your Heavenly Father says you are "happy," and you are "fortunate." These words are not changeable like the weather, one day hot, one day cold. They are from the voice of the One who said, *"Heaven and earth will disappear, but My words will never disappear."* (Matthew 24:25) As Bill Gothard wrote, *"It's His blessing alone that makes our lives what they were meant to be, and we can't be satisfied until we have it."*[1]

Wherever you go and whatever you do, you will be blessed.[2] *Blessed are those who trust in the Lord and have made the Lord their hope and confidence.*[3] *How we praise God, the Father of our Lord Jesus Christ, who has blessed us with every spiritual blessing in the heavenly realms because we belong to Christ.*[4] *God Himself has blessed you forever.*[5]

References:
[1]The Power of Spoken Blessings
[2]Deuteronomy 28:6; [3]Jeremiah 17:7
[4]Ephesians 1:3; [5]Psalm 45:2

Your Name
FAVORED

One definition given by Webster's Dictionary for the word FAVOR is PROVIDING PREFERENTIAL TREATMENT. We all love to be treated with preference.

Do you find it hard to believe God favors you and gives you preferential treatment? Or do you say, "I don't deserve God's favor"? Your feelings are not a qualifying factor to receive God's favor. You have the choice to believe and accept these promises as truth by faith in the One who loves us and gave Himself as a sacrifice for us. (Ephesians 5:2)

Like a large shield, You surround them with your favor.[1] Then you will find favor with both God and people.[2] You have granted me life and favor, and Your care has preserved my spirit.[3] But whatever I am now, it is all because God poured out His special favor on me.[4] "For I look favorably on you, and I know you by name.[5] You who are highly favored! The Lord is with you![6]

References:
[1]Psalm 5:12; [2]Proverbs 3:4
[3]Job 10:12 (KJV); [4]1 Corinthians 15:10
[5]Exodus 33:17; [6]Luke 1:28b (NIV)

Your Name
LOVED

Love and trust are the basis of any successful relationship. As Pastor John Bradshaw stated, "You can trust Someone whom you know loves you completely. You can feel safe with Somebody whom you know loves you completely. And you can love Somebody whom you know loves you with no strings attached, which is why the Bible says, *"We love Him, because He first loved us".*[4] God offers you love that compares to no other."

I love you with an everlasting love.[2] *It's obvious how much He loves me.*[3] *But God is rich in mercy because of His great love for us.*[4] *And God our Father, who loved us and by His grace gave us eternal comfort and a wonderful hope.*[5] *And I am convinced that nothing can ever separate us from God's love. Neither death nor life, neither angels nor demons, neither our fears for today nor our worries about tomorrow—not even the powers of hell can separate us from God's love.*[6]

References:
[1]1 John 4:19 (KJV); [2]Jeremiah 31:3 (GW)
[3]Song of Solomon 2:4; [4]Ephesians 2:4 (GW)
[5]2 Thessalonians 2:16; [6]Romans 8:38

Your Name
AMBASSADOR

Good news deserves to be shared. Now that you understand the loving names your Heavenly Fathers calls you, do you know someone who needs to hear this good news? Scripture calls us AMBASSADORS. One definition of the word ambassador given by Webster's Dictionary is AN OFFICIAL REPRESENTATIVE OF THE HIGHEST RANK. When Jesus healed the man possessed by demons, He instructed him to go and share the good news:

"Go home to your family, and tell them everything the Lord has done for you and how merciful He has been." (Mark 5:19) When Paul the Apostle was healed, Ananias' words to him from Jesus were, "For you are to be His witness, telling everyone what you have seen and heard." (Acts 22:15) David received great forgiveness and restoration and made a vow that, "Your awe-inspiring deeds will be on every tongue; I will proclaim Your greatness." (Psalms 145:6)

Will you join me as an "official representative" in proclaiming the good news? Then, go and share these "awe-inspiring" words you have heard.

Reference:
So we are Christ's ambassadors.
(2 Corinthians 5:20)

The Greatest
INVITATION

The greatest relationship you will ever experience is a personal relationship with Jesus Christ. His invitation to healing, forgiveness, deliverance, peace, and restoration can be yours. The One who calls you special, precious, treasured, and beloved, loves you beyond measure. Here is a prayer I prayed, and my life has never been the same. You have the choice of saying the same from the bottom of your heart today:

Father, You have promised that if I confess my sin, You will forgive me and cleanse me from all the wrong I have done (1 John 1:9). I confess now. Forgive me. Fill me with your Holy Spirit. I accept every name You have called me. Take my hand and walk with me for the rest of my life. In Jesus' name, amen.

About the AUTHOR

As an author and speaker, Merle M. Mills, founder of *Changed Through the Word*, ministers throughout the Hampton Roads area sharing the good news of a changed life through words from the Holy Scriptures. Her prayer is that her reading and listening audience will allow the power of the ever-living God the freedom to do the same in and through their lives.

Her book, *No More a Secret: A Guide to Healing After Abortion*, and the accompanying CD, *No More a Secret*, bring hope and healing to women, especially those experiencing after-abortion trauma. Her recent books, *Hand in Hand with the Master*, a 31-day devotional featuring poetry, Scripture, and words of encouragement, and *You Are Forgiven* have also brought hope and encouragement to many.

Merle resides with her family in Norfolk, Virginia.

Changed Through the Word
P. O. Box 41293
Norfolk, VA 23541

www.changedthrutheword.org
www.changedthrutheword.blogspot.com
www.nomoreasecret.blogspot.com
email: changedthrutheword@gmail.com

www.ingramcontent.com/pod-product-compliance
Lightning Source LLC
Chambersburg PA
CBHW070112070426
42448CB00038B/2583